CW01500328

Original title:
Oaken Hues Within the Faerie Husk

Author: Johan Kirsipuu
ISBN HARDBACK: 978-1-80562-893-4
ISBN PAPERBACK: 978-1-80564-414-9

Murmurs of Past Lives in Lush Wilderness

In the forest where secrets breathe,
Whispers dance beneath the leaves,
Echoes of dreams long since lost,
A tapestry woven, no matter the cost.

Moss carpets the paths of time,
Each step a memory, subtle and sublime,
Nature's embrace, a gentle guide,
Leading wanderers where shadows abide.

Beneath the boughs, old stories reside,
Of lovers, heroes, those who once cried,
Their laughter a melody, soft yet clear,
Carried on breezes, still drawing near.

The brook babbles secrets to stones,
As flora bloom in vibrant tones,
In every petal, a tale retold,
Of spirits entwined, both timid and bold.

As twilight descends, stars start to gleam,
The wilderness hums with a lingering dream,
In the hush of the night, you may find,
The murmurs of past lives, forever entwined.

Glades of Wonder Beneath the Celestial Canopy

In glades where shadows gently fall,
The whispers of the nightbirds call.
Moonlit paths of silver gleam,
A place where dreams and starlight beam.

Beneath the canopy, secrets lie,
The dance of fireflies in the sky.
Nature's magic softly flows,
In every breeze, a story grows.

Through tangled vines, the laughter sings,
Of ancient tales and enchanted things.
The roots entwine in silent pact,
While gentle streams keep secrets intact.

With every step, the heart takes flight,
In wonder's realm, bathed in light.
The trees stand guard, strong and wise,
Their branches stretching to the skies.

So find your way through this lush land,
Where every moment feels so grand.
In glades of wonder, let time cease,
Embrace the magic, bask in peace.

Melodies of Light Between the Leaves

Between the leaves, a whisper flows,
A serenade where sunlight glows.
The rustling grass and sighing streams,
Compose a symphony of dreams.

Each note a ripple, soft and clear,
A melody that draws you near.
The sunlight dances on the floor,
As nature's music calls for more.

In this realm, the shadows play,
As birds announce the break of day.
With every rustle, secrets wake,
The heart attunes, the spirit aches.

Yet in the quiet, whispers reign,
A harmony entwined with pain.
For every joy, there's sorrow's song,
In nature's cradle, we belong.

So linger here where music flows,
In gentle waves, where magic glows.
Between the leaves, let time unfold,
In melodies of light, be bold.

The Faerie's Chorus in Leafy Chapels

In leafy chapels, faeries dwell,
Their laughter rings like silver bell.
With wings of gossamer and grace,
They weave enchantments in this space.

The blossoms sway, as if in dance,
While every creature takes a chance.
To join the chorus of delight,
In twilight's glow, beneath the night.

Their whispers echo, soft and sweet,
In every turn, a rhythmic beat.
The petals shimmer, bathed in dreams,
Where magic flows in gentle streams.

Through emerald aisles, the shadows play,
As faerie lights chase dusk away.
Their songs are secrets, tender, old,
A symphony of stories told.

So step with care in this thrumming heart,
Where nature's wonders never part.
In leafy chapels, let souls soar,
In faerie's chorus, forevermore.

Mysteries of Nature's Golden Gaze

Beneath the trees, where shadows lie,
The golden gaze of sun drifts by.
A tapestry of warmth and light,
Unfolding secrets, pure and bright.

In every rustle, tales arise,
From whispered leaves to open skies.
Each creature moves in playful dance,
In nature's realm, we're caught, entranced.

The brook's soft murmur, pure and clear,
Holds mysteries for those who hear.
While flickers of the sunlight play,
A golden thread through night and day.

So pause awhile, and close your eyes,
Feel all the wonder that underlies.
In nature's gaze, the answers lay,
Whispered softly in a golden spray.

For in this world of lush embrace,
We find our truth, our sacred place.
As nature breathes her heartfelt sigh,
We are but dreams that never die.

Beneath the Canopy of Starlit Wishes

Underneath the shimmering night,
Dreams take flight on wings of light.
Each star whispers secrets old,
Stories of wishes not yet told.

Shadows dance in gentle sway,
Guiding hope along the way.
Moonbeams weave a silver thread,
Where whispered wishes find their bed.

A lone owl calls, its voice so clear,
An echo of magic we hold dear.
In this calm, our hearts unite,
Beneath the vast and wondrous night.

Fireflies waltz in golden streams,
Chasing the glow of starlit dreams.
With every flicker, hope proclaims,
The world is filled with bright new flames.

So let our spirits rise and soar,
To bask in light forevermore.
For in this glow, our fears are eased,
Beneath the starlit canopy, we're pleased.

Phantoms of Light in Ancient Glades

In the woods where shadows creep,
Ancient glades wake from their sleep.
Light spills softly on the ground,
In this dusk, the phantoms abound.

Silhouettes of trees so tall,
Guard the secrets, keep them all.
Whispers echo through the leaves,
Stories told in hushed reprieves.

Ghostly beams through branches weave,
Revealing paths where few believe.
Each step taken, a tale untold,
In the realm where dreams unfold.

With every rustle, a promise glows,
Of hidden worlds where magic flows.
Phantoms dance in twilight's breath,
Celebrating life beyond mere death.

Among the ferns, there lies a spark,
A flicker shining through the dark.
In this light, fear yields to bliss,
Finding peace in every mist.

Chronicles of Enchantment in Woven Roots

Within the earth, where magic sleeps,
Whispers rise from ancient deeps.
Roots embrace the tales of old,
Chronicles of wonders bold.

Threads of time in each embrace,
Nature's weavings leave a trace.
In the soil, enchantments grow,
A tapestry of dreams aglow.

With gentle hands, the seasons spin,
Stories of joy, of loss, of sin.
Every turn, a fate entwined,
In the heart of every mind.

Echoes linger in the air,
Talking trees in their quiet lair.
Listen close, and you might find,
Secrets held, both bright and blind.

In the forest, a soft refrain,
Calls us back to where we've lain.
In woven roots, we are embraced,
By history's hand, our souls interlaced.

The Heart's Breath Among the Celestial Trees

In the grove where starlight streams,
Hope ignites and softly gleams.
Celestial trees, proud and tall,
Hear the heartbeat of us all.

Leaves of silver, whispers sweet,
Bend with grace where spirits meet.
Each pulse carries a wish anew,
A promise shared between the few.

Beneath the bows, our dreams take flight,
Floating softly into the night.
Crickets sing in harmony,
A lullaby of destiny.

The heart's breath echoes through the air,
A song of love beyond compare.
In this hush, we find our peace,
Among the trees, our worries cease.

With every rustle, nature calls,
A gentle pull, a magic thralls.
In this sanctuary, we belong,
Where silence wraps us in its song.

Fables Carved in Mossy Embrace

In shadows deep, the stories lie,
Carved in moss, where whispers sigh.
Old stones tell tales of dreams long past,
Of ancient woods and shadows cast.

Beneath the boughs, the creatures roam,
In the twilight's mist, they call it home.
Fables spin like leaves in flight,
A dance of life, both dark and bright.

With every rustle, secrets blend,
In nature's arms, where stories mend.
The air is thick with magic's breath,
A silent hymn that speaks of death.

As twilight weaves its silken thread,
The ancient ones rise from the dead.
Their laughter echoes, soft and clear,
A timeless song for those who hear.

So seek the grove where wild winds play,
And let the fables guide your way.
For in the mossy embrace you'll find,
The whispers of an ageless mind.

The Dance of Sylphs Underneath the Twilight

Underneath the twilight's gaze,
Sylphs gather for their secret ways.
Whirling lightly on the breeze,
They beckon hearts to join with ease.

With shimmering wings like golden light,
They twirl and spin through the velvet night.
Each step a breath of wild delight,
A dance of dreams, a wondrous sight.

The stars above lend gentle grace,
As sylphs entwine in soft embrace.
They whisper tales of worlds unseen,
Of magic spun in glistening green.

Through silvered woods and crystal streams,
They flit like echoes of vibrant dreams.
In every sigh, a promise made,
A fleeting glimpse of light that fades.

So watch them dance in the dusk's warm glow,
Underneath the twilight, where secrets flow.
For in their rhythm, life takes flight,
Beneath the canopy of soft moonlight.

Elven Serenades in the Heart of the Grove

In the heart of the grove, where echoes play,
Elven songs weave night and day.
With voices bright like morning dew,
They sing of love, forever true.

Through tangled roots and ancient bark,
Their melodies flicker, a vibrant spark.
Each note a whisper, soft and sweet,
Awakening the world beneath their feet.

With laughter ringing through the trees,
They dance along with the breeze.
Their silver hair a flowing stream,
In twilight's haze, a waking dream.

The moon bears witness, pale and bright,
To elven revels in the night.
Each serenade a tale retold,
Of heroes brave and lovers bold.

So linger long where shadows dwell,
And listen close to their sweet spell.
In every harmony, a voice so pure,
Elven hearts, forever endure.

Secrets of the Enchanted Woodland Veil

Beyond the veil of wooded dreams,
Where sunlight dances, and magic gleams,
Lie secrets known to the ancient trees,
A world that whispers upon the breeze.

In every rustling leaf, a tale,
Of fae and spirits that never fail.
Their laughter echoes through the night,
A serenade of pure delight.

With shadows weaving a mystic game,
The woodland glows with a fiery flame.
Each pathway leads to a hidden lore,
Where time stands still forevermore.

So venture forth, let curiosity lead,
For in the wild lies every seed.
The secrets flourish, like blossoms rare,
In the enchanted veil, waiting there.

And if you find the heart's true call,
The woodland's magic will not let fall.
For every moment spent in grace,
Holds the pulse of the earth's embrace.

A Tapestry Woven Under Starry Canopies

In twilight's glow, the night unfolds,
A tapestry of dreams and tales,
Where whispered secrets softly mold,
And moonlit paths weave through the gales.

Each star a story, brightly ignites,
The echoes of the past collide,
With silver threads that dance in flights,
Beneath the vast, celestial tide.

A canopy where shadows play,
The branches cradle voices kind,
As shadows weave the night's ballet,
In peace, their gentle songs unwind.

With every twinkle in the dark,
A spark of magic fills the air,
As stardust paints a timeless mark,
And blankets dreams with tender care.

So rest beneath this vaulted sky,
Where slumber weaves its softest thread,
For in the night, our spirits fly,
In stories shared, where none are wed.

Luminous Fables in the Depths of the Wild

In the heart of forests deep and vast,
Luminous fables start to weave,
With whispers of the future cast,
In shadows where the wild things breathe.

Amongst the ferns and ancient trees,
The tales of old begin to twine,
With every rustle in the breeze,
A language rich, divine, and fine.

Glowing orbs of light take flight,
As creatures dance in silver glow,
Their stories carried through the night,
In secret paths where few may go.

The soft embrace of twilight's grace,
Invites us to the sacred lore,
Where freedom blooms in every space,
And nature sings forevermore.

A woodland world, where dreams awake,
In fables shared beneath the trees,
Each shimmering moment, fate will take,
In harmony with wild decrees.

Where Nature's Spirit Sings in Harmony

Where rivers run and mountains rise,
Nature's spirit sings anew,
In songs of winds beneath the skies,
And echoes dance, both bright and true.

With every petal, every leaf,
A symphony of life unfolds,
In joy and sorrow, sweet and brief,
The heart of nature, warm and bold.

The rustling grass, the chirping birds,
Compose a melody divine,
In harmony, beyond mere words,
A tapestry of hope entwined.

Beneath the boughs, where shadows play,
A lullaby of earth and sun,
In every dawn, in every day,
Life blooms with magic, never done.

So listen closely, hearts align,
In nature's chorus, find your place,
For in her song, a love divine,
Awaits in every sweet embrace.

Tales Spun in the Heart of the Woodland

In the heart of woodlands, shadows blend,
Tales spun from whispers, soft and low,
Where ancient secrets gently send,
A magic woven, ebb and flow.

With every step on leaf-strewn path,
The stories of the forest rise,
In gentle laughter, nature's math,
A symphony of earth, so wise.

The brook's soft babble, mossy nook,
Hold echoes of the past's embrace,
In every tree and cranny, look,
For wonders found in timeless grace.

As twilight drapes her velvet shroud,
The woodland glimmers, softly bright,
Where every creature, small and loud,
Adds to the mystery of the night.

So linger long where shadows dwell,
In tales spun deep, let heart explore,
For in the magic, we can tell,
The woodland waits, forevermore.

Reverberations of Lost Dreams in Green Corridors

In corridors where whispers weave,
Soft echoes rise like morning breath.
Dreams that dance on leaves of jade,
Fade to shadows, lost in depths.

Beneath the boughs where time stands still,
Fragrant memories burst and bloom.
A tapestry of hopes once spun,
Now woven tight in silent gloom.

In every step, the past remains,
A gentle tug on heartstrings tight.
Through tangled paths, the spirit strains,
To grasp what shimmers just from sight.

Yet in the silence, voices call,
Inviting souls to reclaim the night.
Hushed spells resound, they rise and fall,
In corridors bathed in twilight.

A promise hangs in air so sweet,
For dreams not lost but waiting near.
In green embrace, we find our feet,
Reverberating hope sincere.

Celestial Meadows and Kamikaze Winds

In meadows bright where stardust falls,
The winds collide with reckless glee.
A cosmic dance, both fierce and free,
Kamikaze whispers, echoing calls.

Celestial blooms in twilight hues,
Unfurl beneath a silver streak.
With every gust, the heavens speak,
Their secrets shared in softest clues.

Each blade of grass, a world untold,
A soft embrace of fate and chance.
In nature's arms, we find romance,
As daring breezes rush and fold.

Yet shadows lurk where joy expands,
A trace of sorrow in the sway.
But every night will yield to day,
In meadows kissed by unseen hands.

So dance, dear heart, in winds so bold,
Let laughter lift you, take your flight.
With constellations shining bright,
Weaving stories long foretold.

Woven Dreams of Fern and Blossom

In emerald groves where ferns do sway,
Dreams are stitched with threads of light.
Blossoms whisper secrets bright,
Crafting tales in shadows play.

The heartbeats thrum, a pulse entwined,
As daylight meets the soft twilight.
With every rustle, hope takes flight,
In nature's hands, our fate defined.

Petals flutter in the breeze,
A fragrant hymn, a sweet refrain.
Each droplet dances, free from pain,
As time retreats, our souls at ease.

Woven dreams among the roots,
Anchor us to earth and sky.
In gentle realms, we learn to fly,
As life unveils its sweetest fruits.

So gather round this sacred space,
Where nature's art entwines our fates.
In fern and blossom, hope awaits,
A tapestry of love and grace.

Glow of Enchantment in the Whispering Wood

In woods where secrets softly sigh,
A glow ignites the ancient trees.
With tendrils curled like whispered pleas,
Enchantment sparkles in the sky.

The leaves confide in murmured tones,
Each rustling breath a story spun.
Underneath the watchful sun,
The heart finds peace, its thirst now sown.

Amidst the shadows, magic seems,
To swirl and twist in playful grace.
A world alive, a warm embrace,
Where every thought converts to dreams.

The night descends with velvet calm,
Yet luminescence weaves through night.
In every corner, sparks ignite,
A gentle spell, a soothing charm.

So wander here, where wonder grows,
And let the woods wrap you in bliss.
In whispered realms, a perfect kiss,
Will echo soft where magic flows.

Reveries in the Heart of Nature's Caress

In the meadow where wildflowers sway,
Sunlight dances on the soft, green clay.
Whispers of wind weave through the trees,
Nature's embrace brings sweet memories.

A brook babbles tales of olden days,
Reflecting the sky in a shimmering blaze.
Beneath the boughs, where shadows play,
Magic awakens, in soft, slow ballet.

The rustle of leaves sings a soft tune,
As the stars make their path in the light of the moon.
Every petal, every stone, a story untold,
In whispers of nature, pure and bold.

Life pulses here in a vibrant array,
From dawn's first blush to the end of the day.
Each creature and plant, in harmony meld,
In nature's caress, our hearts are held.

So let us wander, with spirits set free,
In this enchanting world, where we long to be.
For in every moment, there's magic to find,
In the heart of nature, our souls intertwined.

Twilight Whispers of Moss and Mist

As twilight descends with a silvery sigh,
Moss carpets the ground 'neath the evening sky.
Mist weaves through branches, a delicate lace,
In whispers of twilight, we find our place.

The call of the owl, a haunting refrain,
Echoes through shadows where secrets remain.
Stars peek through clouds, a soft, gentle light,
Guiding our hearts on this tender night.

The world feels enchanted, alive with the glow,
Of memories hidden, of dreams yet to flow.
Each flicker of firefly, a wish unconfined,
In the hush of the night, new paths we can find.

With every soft breath, we savor the peace,
In the fold of the dusk, our worries release.
As nature surrounds us, a comforting gift,
In twilight's embrace, our spirits uplift.

So linger a moment, let time gently pause,
In moss and in mist, we find our own cause.
For in this stillness, our hearts softly beat,
In twilight's whispers, life feels complete.

The Sylvan Spirit's Gentle Breath

In a realm where the wildflowers bloom,
The sylvan spirit dances, dispelling the gloom.
With laughter like raindrops, it flutters and twirls,
Bringing joy to the forest, where magic unfurls.

Through thickets and glades, its presence is felt,
In the rustling leaves, where the sunlight has knelt.
Each whispering breeze carries tales of old,
Of adventures and wonders, both timid and bold.

The murmur of streams in a soft, soothing hymn,
Echoes the spirit's song, gentle and slim.
As shadows grow long, and the day starts to fade,
The forest awakens, in colors displayed.

Each creature that scurries, each fluttering wing,
Is a part of the harmony the sylvan does bring.
In every soft heartbeat that stirs in the night,
The essence of nature glows ever so bright.

So take a moment, breathe deeply the air,
Feel the spirit's embrace, a soft, loving care.
In the heart of the woods, let your worries flee,
For the sylvan spirit sings, wild and free.

Tangle of Roots and Mirthful Dreams

In a realm where the roots tangle deep,
Mirthful dreams slumber, in silence they keep.
Each branch tells a tale, each leaf has a song,
In this sanctuary, where we all belong.

Beneath ancient oaks, where shadows entwine,
Whispers of stories like aged, sweet vine.
The laughter of children, in echoes resound,
As they dance through the forest, where magic is found.

The brook's gentle giggle, a playful delight,
Weaves through the grasses, a shimmering light.
In the heart of the woods, where wishes take flight,
The tangle of roots leads to dreams every night.

With every sweet breath of the soft, rustling air,
Each moment awakens a memory rare.
The wonder of nature, a tapestry grand,
Where mirthful dreams twinkle, like grains of sand.

So wander with wonder, let your heart dream wide,
In the tangle of roots, let your spirit abide.
For in every heartbeat, in every soft sigh,
Lies the essence of nature, where souls learn to fly.

Flickering Lights of the Woodland Utopia

In the forest where soft whispers reside,
Flickering lights dance, lovingly allied.
Beneath the branches, shadows play,
A luminous tapestry woven in clay.

Mossy carpets beneath our feet,
Nature's symphony, wild and sweet.
The stars seem to laugh in this tranquil space,
An invitation to dream, a warm embrace.

Creatures of myth, in silence they roam,
Each flicker of light, a glimpse of home.
Wings of the night draw paths in the dark,
Guiding lost souls towards a gentle spark.

The moon gazes down, a watchful eye,
While secrets in shadows begin to fly.
With every heartbeat, magic ignites,
In the flickering lights of the woodland nights.

Pathways of Memory in the Fairies' Glade

Where the willows sway, time takes its flight,
In the fairies' glade, cloaked in soft light.
Pathways of memory, whispering dreams,
Echoes of laughter in shimmering streams.

Petals like whispers brush against skin,
Guiding the heart where the journey begins.
With each gentle breeze, they twirl and they sway,
A dance of enchantment that beckons to stay.

Veils of mist shroud the secrets untold,
Stories of wonder, forever enfold.
Nestled in petals, the past intertwines,
Painting our memories with magical lines.

Beneath silver skies, we frolic and play,
In the fairies' glade, where dreams find their way.
The moon's gentle glow holds memories tight,
Eternal enchantment, through day and through night.

The Pulse of the Forest in Swirling Shadows

In shadows that swirl, the forest awakes,
A heartbeat resounds as the silence breaks.
Roots intertwine, ancient and wise,
Telling their stories beneath sprawling skies.

Through rustling leaves, a cadence is heard,
Soft murmurs of life, in each whispered word.
The pulse of the forest, a rhythm unique,
Guides wandering souls to the paths that they seek.

Where sunlight and starlight entwine in a dance,
We surrender to magic, surrender to chance.
The songs of the night play sweet symphonies,
In the heart of the woodland, carried by breeze.

Amidst swirling shadows, enchantment prevails,
Stories of old on soft, twilight trails.
In the pulse of the forest, each breath we take,
Connects us to life, the memories we make.

Chasing Echoes in the Enchanted Arbor

Beneath the boughs of the enchanted arbor,
We chase echoes of laughter and the light they borrow.
A place where time drifts like twinkling dust,
In the magic of moments, we place our trust.

The whispers of trees sway stories so grand,
Their roots entrenched in this mystical land.
With every step taken, the world starts to hum,
While echoes of wonder begin to come undone.

Sunbeams dance lightly on petals and leaves,
In a symphony crafted, our heartaches reprieves.
With joy like the breeze, we leap and we twirl,
In the enchanted arbor, we dream and we whirl.

As twilight descends and shadows grow long,
We trace the soft echoes of nature's own song.
Chasing the remnants of laughter and cheer,
In the enchanted arbor, forever we'll steer.

Secrets Wrapped in Twilight's Veil

In twilight's hush, where whispers spin,
A world of dreams begins to win.
Veils of shadow, secrets fold,
Their tales of wonder softly told.

With stars alight in velvet skies,
The moon unveils her silver guise.
Each breeze a song, each rustle clear,
A circle formed when night draws near.

From ancient trees, the stories sigh,
Of magic lost, of days gone by.
In hidden glades, the fae do dance,
Entwined in fate, in timeless chance.

The mist wraps round like a loving shroud,
A cloak of night, serene and proud.
And in this realm, so deep, so wide,
Life's secrets in the shadows bide.

So linger here, in twilight's grip,
Where every moment holds a quip.
In twilight's veil, our spirits soar,
And find the tales worth longing for.

Sylvan Shadows and Mystical Lights

Among the trees where shadows play,
Mystical lights dance through the day.
They twirl and gleam, in pools of gold,
Revealing tales of ages old.

The forest breathes its ancient lore,
With every step, you'll yearn for more.
Beneath the boughs, in every nook,
Lives every fable in a book.

The soft caress of mossy ground,
With echoes of a world profound.
Each flicker shows what lie ahead,
In sylvan dreams where few have tread.

Night casts a veil, and stars ignite,
Bathing the woods in gentle light.
In whispered winds, there's magic pure,
A bond of nature, strong and sure.

So let your heart be wild and free,
Within these woods, the key to see.
Sylvan shadows and lights entwined,
In every corner, answers find.

The Lure of the Verdant Shroud

The verdant shroud, so rich and deep,
Calls out to wanderers who seek.
Beneath the leaves, where secrets nest,
A world unfolds, a nature's jest.

From emerald glades, the laughter spills,
As brooklets sing o'er verdant hills.
Each footstep leads where dreams reside,
In nature's arms, there's naught to hide.

The sunbeams wane, the shadows grow,
In tangled roots where wild things flow.
A spirit calls, a soft refrain,
In whispers sweet like summer rain.

Each path a tale, each breeze a sigh,
Inviting souls to soar and fly.
The verdant shroud, a warm embrace,
In nature's heart, we find our place.

So venture forth, let go your fears,
In lush embrace, the world appears.
The lure of green will hold you tight,
In every shadow, joy ignites.

Ethereal Glow of Leafy Realms

In leafy realms where whispers bloom,
An ethereal glow dispels the gloom.
Beneath the canopies, dreams ignite,
With every breath, the spirits light.

The gentle sway of boughs above,
Hides wonders that call forth our love.
In dappled shade, the faeries play,
Revealing secrets of the day.

A tapestry of life unfolds,
In vibrant hues and stories told.
Through singing leaves, the magic flows,
In every heart, the nature knows.

The dusk descends, a velvet wrap,
In emerald shadows, the stars map.
Each twinkle hints at distant sights,
An invitation to chase the lights.

So linger here, in twilight's grace,
Let nature's pulse your heart embrace.
In leafy realms, your spirit sings,
Awakening the joy that springs.

Charmed Silhouettes in the Moonlight

In the glow of silver skies,
Whispers dance on twilight's breath.
Shadows weave with dreams that rise,
In the quiet of night's caress.

Wands of willow gently sway,
Underneath the lunar gleam.
Creatures frolic, spirits play,
Crafting wonders, as they dream.

Echoes of a soft, sweet song,
Bounce upon the velvet air.
Time slips by, the world feels strong,
Filled with magic everywhere.

Mystic paths of sapphire light,
Guide the hearts that dare to roam.
Crossing thresholds of the night,
Finding peace, they call it home.

With each heartbeat, tales unfold,
Secrets held in every sigh.
In the moonlight, brave and bold,
Charmed silhouettes dance and fly.

Gilded Leaves in the Realm of Whimsy

In a forest draped in gold,
Leaves of laughter catch the sun.
Winds of fortune brave and bold,
Whisper secrets, tales begun.

Squirrels chuckle, stars alight,
In the branches, sunlight weaves.
Every moment feels just right,
Glimmers dance among the leaves.

Bubbling brooks hum a tune,
Soothing hearts that wander near.
Magic sparkles, afternoon,
Where wonder banishes fear.

Here, in playful echoes found,
Imagination takes its flight.
With each step upon the ground,
Charmed adventures come to light.

In this realm where dreams can roam,
Gilded leaves whisper and twirl.
Every heart can find a home,
In the magic of this world.

Veils of Enchantment in Nature's Embrace

Through the mist, a soft embrace,
Nature whispers in the grove.
Veils of magic, gentle grace,
Wrap the world in twilight's love.

Color blooms in twilight's gleam,
Where the river finds its peace.
Every leaf and flower gleams,
Carrying the whispers' lease.

Stars come forth to play their part,
Guiding dreams beneath their light.
In the stillness, beats a heart,
Filled with wonder, pure delight.

Every shadow, every sound,
Tells a story, soft and sweet.
In this paradise unbound,
Joy and beauty gently meet.

Embrace the calm, the soft night air,
Let the fireflies cast their glow.
In this moment, free of care,
Veils of enchantment softly flow.

The Sorcery of Sylphs and Sprites

In the meadows, wild and free,
Sylphs take flight on gentle breeze.
With a flicker, they watch me,
Beneath the ancient, whispering trees.

Sprites burst forth from flowers' light,
Sharing laughter, soft and pure.
Underneath the starry night,
They weave dreams, a magic cure.

Petals sway with every laugh,
As moonbeams sprinkle love around.
Every dance, a cherished craft,
In this world where dreams are found.

Listen close to nature's song,
Feel the rhythm in your heart.
Here, where you truly belong,
Sorcery's gentle art.

With a wink and playful sigh,
Moments vanish, joy takes flight.
In the whispers of the sky,
Sylphs and sprites make magic bright.

Whispers of Enchanted Timber

In the forest deep, where shadows play,
The trees converse in a gentle sway.
A melody of leaves, a choir of night,
Guarding secrets, hidden from sight.

Among the roots, the spirits dance,
In moonlit glades, they take their chance.
With laughter soft, they weave their spell,
In every nook, a tale to tell.

The breeze carries whispers, old and wise,
As stars peek through the velvet skies.
Each twig and branch holds stories untold,
Of magic and wonder, timeless and bold.

A troll may grin by a babbling brook,
While fairies flutter like pages in a book.
With each rustle, the night holds its breath,
In enchanted timber, defying death.

So wander close where the shadows weave,
And let your heart among them believe.
For in every rustling leaf you find,
The echoes of dreams, so beautifully intertwined.

Luminous Glades of Forgotten Dreams

In a glade where light dares to break,
The dreams of the lost begin to wake.
Misty tendrils caress the air,
Guiding the soul with gentle care.

Golden beams filter through the leaves,
As time unwinds, the heart believes.
Whispers of wishes, buried so deep,
In luminous glades, forever to keep.

Past voices linger, soft as a sigh,
Each crevice holds a memory nigh.
Faint echoes shimmer like the dew,
Mapping the hopes that once felt true.

The wildflowers bloom with colors bright,
Painting the canvas of the night.
An ethereal glow, a painter's dream,
In every flicker, life's hidden theme.

So tread lightly where the spirits roam,
In luminous glades, the past finds home.
A tapestry woven in soft twilight,
Guided by stars, and the silver light.

Secrets Woven in Woodland Shadows

In the woodland shadows where mysteries dwell,
Secrets are whispered, a magical spell.
The twilight embraces, a velvet embrace,
Hiding the wonders of time and space.

Every rustle and creak holds a tale,
Of creatures that wander, of dreams set sail.
Beneath the boughs, the stories unfold,
In shadows alive, both timid and bold.

The moonlight dances on leaves so fair,
Revealing the secrets hidden with care.
From the glen to the brook, each turn you take,
Unveils the fabric of magic awake.

A fox may dart with eyes aglow,
While owls serenade the world below.
Every whisper, a memory's thread,
Binding the living with those who've fled.

So listen closely, and you may find,
The echoes of magic that linger behind.
In woodland shadows, let go of your fears,
For the heart knows the truths wrapped in years.

Emerald Canopies and Glistening Dew

Under emerald canopies, life takes flight,
Where the morning dew sparkles with light.
In the hush of dawn, each drop a gem,
Reflecting the dreams within the diadem.

The leaves whisper secrets, soft and low,
As the gentle wind begins to blow.
Nestled in green, the world feels new,
As nature's canvas, painted in hue.

Through tangled vines and branches wide,
Each creature scurries, where shadows hide.
In the glistening dew, stories unite,
A tapestry woven by morning's light.

A squirrel's chatter, the song of the stream,
In emerald realms, life flows like a dream.
With every heartbeat, the forest sings,
A ballad of hope that the daylight brings.

So wander forth, where the wild things roam,
In emerald canopies, you'll find your home.
Among the dew-kissed leaves, feel the embrace,
Of nature's enchantment, a timeless place.

Hymns Sung by the Oldest Trees

In shadows deep where whispers dwell,
The ancient trees weave tales to tell.
With roots that stretch through time and space,
They sing of life, of love's embrace.

Their leaves, like choir, in breezes sway,
An ode to night, a hymn to day.
With bark like pages of stories old,
Each knot a secret, each ring a gold.

They herald storms and gentle rain,
Through tempest wild, through joy and pain.
Their limbs extend to skies so wide,
In grace, they dance with earthly pride.

A melody of years gone by,
The rustle speaks, the branches sigh.
In every bough, a memory lingers,
In nature's heart, weave life with fingers.

So gather 'round, both young and old,
The stories shared, the wisdom bold.
The oldest trees, they know the way,
With hymns of time, they'll lead our stay.

Elysian Woodlands and Evening's Glow

In twilight's grace where shadows play,
The woodlands breathe, a soft ballet.
With colors brushed in golden hue,
The evening stirs, bids day adieu.

Beneath the boughs of emerald green,
A magical world, serene, unseen.
The fireflies blink in soft delight,
Awakening dreams with twinkling light.

Each path we take, in silence, glows,
With secrets only the moonlight knows.
The whispers of the night surround,
In each soft rustle, a mystic sound.

As crickets sing a lullaby,
The stars peek out, the world awry.
In this embrace of night's design,
The heart finds peace, the soul aligns.

So wander here, where wonders lie,
Among the trees, beneath the sky.
In Elysian woods, let spirits flow,
And lose yourself in evening's glow.

Secrets hidden in the Cradle of Green

In emerald depths where shadows rest,
The cradle holds the nature's best.
With gentle sighs and curls of mist,
Secrets awaken, in silence kissed.

The ferns unfurl in tender grace,
Each leaf a tale, a sacred space.
The flowers whisper in hues so rare,
Of love's first bloom, of life laid bare.

Beneath the surface, stories creep,
The earth remembers, the silence keeps.
In roots entwined, a history grows,
Of ancient knowing, of timeless flows.

The brook babbles softly, a murmured tune,
Reflecting the dance of sun and moon.
In every droplet, a secret waits,
In the cradle of green, where magic pervades.

So find the path where shadows gleam,
The hidden truths, the whispered dream.
In nature's arms, let your heart be seen,
In the secrets held in the cradle of green.

Horizon of Chance Beneath the Branches

Beneath the branches, fate entwines,
A tapestry spun with silver lines.
Each moment waits, a chance to take,
In whispered breaths the earth shall wake.

With every rustle, new beginnings bloom,
As sunlight dances, dispelling gloom.
The horizon stretches, a canvas wide,
Where hopes take flight, in dreams abide.

The forest breathes, alive with chance,
In every turn, there's room to dance.
With every step upon the ground,
The wonders of the world abound.

So wander forth, with heart prepared,
For treasures found and burdens shared.
In every glance beneath the tree,
A horizon of chance awaits for thee.

Let laughter echo through the glade,
And chase the shadows, be unafraid.
For beneath the branches, life will show,
A panorama vast where spirits flow.

Chronicles of Light Amidst the Elder Trees

In the heart of the woods, where shadows dance,
Whispers of secrets take every chance.
Moonlight shimmered on branches gnarled,
As ancient tales from the past were heralded.

Children of dawn with laughter bright,
Chasing the sparkles that twinkled in flight.
Elder trees bowed low in grace,
Guardians of dreams, a mystical place.

Golden leaves flutter, twinkling like stars,
Carrying messages from realms afar.
Through tangled roots, the stories thread,
Of heroes courageous and legends dead.

Hidden beneath the emerald veil,
Fragments of magic narrate a tale.
Echoes of friendship, bold and clear,
Shaping the future, erasing the fear.

With each footstep, the light takes its form,
Creating a bond, both tender and warm.
In the twilight's hush, the truth can be found,
Amidst the elder trees, hope knows no bound.

Nightfall Melodies under the Canopied Sky

When twilight hushes the bustling day,
And stars begin their gentle ballet.
A symphony rises from shadowed glades,
Nature's chorus, in soft serenades.

Whispering winds through leaves that sway,
Notes of enchantment beckon to stay.
Crickets take stage with their rhythmic song,
In harmony with the owl's hoot, strong.

The silver moon spills its glow on the ground,
Bathed in magic, the night feels profound.
Each rustling branch sings a lullaby,
As dreams take flight, like sparks in the sky.

Among the shadows, the faeries twirl,
Glimmers of laughter in a mystical whirl.
With every flicker, a story unfolds,
In whispers of night, where wonder beholds.

As the moonlight wanes, new dreams arise,
Painting the heavens with colorful skies.
Nightfall melodies softly imbue,
A tapestry woven with magic anew.

Fragments of Magic in the Bark's Embrace

Beneath the canopy, roots intertwine,
Nature's embrace, steadfast and divine.
Each gnarled trunk holds a memory bright,
Fragments of magic hidden from sight.

Mossy carpets cradle each worn path,
Where echoes of laughter chase after wrath.
In every groove, a story it keeps,
Of whispered wishes and secrets it reaps.

The sun may fade, but shadows ignite,
In the heartbeat of woods, there's absolute light.
For the bark tells tales of hearts so bold,
In every ring, a lifetime unfolds.

Glimmers of wisdom in whispers old,
In the ancient boughs, a treasure untold.
With every heartbeat, the magic remains,
In the souls who wander, in joyous refrains.

From the bark's embrace, dreams take their flight,
Through tangled enchantment, into the night.
The fragments of magic, they twine and lace,
In the world's embrace, we find our place.

The Symphony of Nature and Faerie Flight

In the glade where the wildflowers bloom,
Nature plays softly, dispelling the gloom.
A symphony weaves through the sapphire skies,
As faeries dance lightly, with laughter that flies.

Buzzing of bees in a bright serenade,
Drawing the nectar where dreams are made.
Every fluttering wing carries delight,
In the tales of the whimsical faerie flight.

Beneath the vast canopy, colors entwine,
Painting the canvas with whispers divine.
Cascading leaves in the breeze do conspire,
To compose a melody that rises like fire.

The brook sings along with a tinkling laugh,
As moonbeams twist into a shimmering path.
In rhythms of nature, we find our heart's beat,
Carried by faeries on wings light and fleet.

So when twilight beckons, step into the song,
With love in your heart, where you belong.
For the symphony blooms in the night sky so bright,
And magic lives on in each faerie flight.

The Breath of Magic in Leaf and Bark

In twilight's hush, where shadows play,
Whispers dance on the breeze at bay.
Through emerald canopies, secrets sigh,
The breath of magic, unseen, awry.

Roots entwined with tales of old,
In every knotted branch, stories unfold.
With gentle rustle, the leaves confide,
Of timeworn spells the ancients tried.

A flicker of light through the branches weaves,
As fairies flit in the dusk, like leaves.
Their laughter echoes in the softening glow,
Awakening dreams we yearn to sow.

Hidden glades where wishes bloom,
In the heart of silence, dispelling gloom.
A shimmer of hope on a silvery track,
In the forest's heart, there's no looking back.

So wander deep where wonders dwell,
In every nook, a magic spell.
Let the essence of nature envelop your soul,
In leaf and bark, feel the magic unroll.

Fabled Paths Through Enchanted Thickets

Where tangled vines entwine with fate,
Fabled paths lay in wait,
Inviting souls to wander far,
Beneath the light of a twinkling star.

In the thicket's embrace, time stands still,
Every corner, a tale to fulfill.
Mossy stones bear witness to lore,
Of ancient journeys and tales of yore.

A flutter of wings, soft and bright,
Guiding us through the velvet night.
Each step forward, a story (to) weave,
In the heart of the thicket, we dare believe.

With every shadow, a promise blooms,
Of hidden treasures in twilight's rooms.
The forest whispers, secrets revealed,
In the thicket's depth, our fate is sealed.

So take a step down that winding lane,
Let the senses guide through joy and pain.
Enchanted thickets, vivid and wide,
Hold fabled paths where dreams abide.

Glimmers of Wonder in the Forest's Core

Deep in the woods where wonders stir,
Glimmers of magic begin to blur.
Dappled sunlight through branches spills,
Unfolding dreams in the whispering hills.

Each ray that dances on the leaf,
Weaves tales of joy, and of grief.
In the hush of the trees, old secrets lie,
Waiting patiently for hearts to try.

With each rustle, a story is spun,
From dawn's soft glow to the day's last run.
In the forest's embrace, let go of fear,
For glimmers of wonder draw ever near.

A brook's gentle song, a soft, sweet tune,
Beneath the watchful gaze of the moon.
In glades where the wildflowers sway,
Our spirits dance, come what may.

So venture forth where the wild things play,
Embrace the magic in every ray.
In the forest's core, life's stories ignite,
With glimmers of wonder in the soft twilight.

The Allure of Moss-Covered Secrets

In mossy realms where shadows dwell,
Lie whispered secrets that time will tell.
Each tuft of green, a guardian stands,
Protecting dreams with tender hands.

Pathways lined with emerald hue,
Lead the wanderer to worlds anew.
Each step careful, each heart aglow,
For moss-covered secrets, the forest will show.

A melody carried by the wind's soft breath,
Resonates deeply, defying death.
In the coolness, the earth hums low,
Hints of enchantment in soft, stolen flow.

The allure of nature, both gentle and bold,
In its embrace, the stories unfold.
With every breath, the wonders unfold,
In moss-covered bundles of magic retold.

So linger a while in this verdant space,
Let your heart dance in nature's grace.
For in these woods, where secrets are sown,
In moss-covered mysteries, you're never alone.

The Faerie's Lament Beneath the Ancient Boughs

In shadows deep where whispers dwell,
The faerie weaves her quiet spell.
With tears that shimmer, soft and bright,
She mourns the loss of fleeting light.

Beneath the boughs, so ancient, wise,
Admired by all who roam the skies.
A tale of love, once vibrant, bold,
Now echoes soft, in hues of gold.

Among the roots of forest lore,
She finds a path to dream once more.
But time, it seems, has flown away,
Leaving her spirit lost in sway.

The stars above, they twinkle still,
Yet darkness grows upon the hill.
A gentle breeze, her only friend,
Whispers secrets that never end.

Oh, faerie dear, with wings so light,
Dance through the shadows, chase the night.
For every sigh beneath the bough,
Reminds us all to live the now.

Glimmers of Mystic Glow Among Starlit Roots

Beneath the stars where shadows creep,
Glimmers awaken from their sleep.
With every flicker, whispers rise,
In harmony with velvet skies.

The roots entwined like stories told,
Each bend and curve a thread of gold.
They weave a tapestry so rare,
Of dreams and wishes whispered there.

The moonlight bathes the woodland floor,
In silver hues forevermore.
A dance of sprites and fireflies,
In swirling patterns 'neath the skies.

Each gentle breath, a promise sweet,
Of magic found in every beat.
The earth's own heart begins to glow,
With tales of old in mystic flow.

So listen close to night's embrace,
For in the dark, there's boundless grace.
With glimmers bright among the roots,
The soul remembers its own truths.

Sylvan Echoes of the Woodland Realm

In sylvan glades where shadows play,
The woodland whispers night and day.
A gentle breeze through branches hums,
A song of life, the forest drums.

Each rustling leaf, a tale retold,
Of love and loss in seasons cold.
The echoes of the creatures' call,
Resound among the trees so tall.

With every step on mossy ground,
The heart beats to the ancient sound.
The watchful stars, their gaze so wise,
Illuminate the nighttime skies.

In secret groves, the fae reside,
In moonlit ponds, their wishes bide.
And when the dawn breaks through the haze,
Life stirs awake to greet the day.

So walk with care, where dreams align,
And find the magic held in time.
For in the echoes, loud and clear,
The woodland speaks, if you can hear.

Gnarled Branches and Ethereal Light

Gnarled branches twist, in dance they sway,
Beneath the dawn, a soft array.
Ethereal light begins to creep,
Awakening the world from sleep.

The forest floor, a carpet green,
Where sunlight spills like liquid sheen.
With every step upon this ground,
A symphony of life is found.

Across the boughs, the shadows play,
In whispers shared with break of day.
The twinkling stars begin to wane,
As morning bursts, releasing rain.

Within this realm of ancient trees,
The heart finds calm, the spirit frees.
Gnarled forms embrace the new day's light,
Transcending time, a wondrous sight.

So wander deep where magic dwells,
And heed the tales that silence tells.
For in the light, through trees so grand,
You'll find the beauty, hand in hand.

Where Time Dances in a Circle of Leaves

In the glade where whispers flee,
Leaves twirl down, like secrets free.
Time spins softly, round it flows,
In everyone's heart, the magic grows.

Beneath the boughs, the children dream,
Of sparkling stars and silver beams.
As shadows stretch and daylight winks,
The world dissolves in gentle blinks.

Old oak watches, rooted and wise,
Guarding echoes of long-lost sighs.
Each rustle tells a tale of yore,
In this realm, forevermore.

Colors shift as dusk draws near,
Embracing laughter, welcoming cheer.
Where time stands still, and hearts believe,
In the dance of leaves, we weave.

So come, dear friend, let spirits tease,
In circles spun on autumn's breeze.
With every whirl, a wish you'll find,
In the leafy waltz, souls intertwined.

Rooted Dreams in the Forest's Heart

Beneath the canopy, dreams take flight,
In shadows deep, where hearts ignite.
Roots entwine beneath the loam,
In this wild place, we find our home.

Silent whispers brush the skin,
Calling forth the quests within.
Trees hold secrets, old and wise,
In their embrace, our spirits rise.

Mossy carpets cradle our feet,
While gentle streams hum soft and sweet.
Roots of hope, our anchor strong,
In the forest, we all belong.

The moonlight filters, silver beams,
Illuminating all our dreams.
With every sigh, the night unveils,
The magic spun in shadowed trails.

So linger here, where wonders blend,
In rooted dreams, let journeys mend.
In forest's heart, where spirits gleam,
We live the truths of every dream.

The Enchantment of Twilight Canopies

As twilight drapes its gentle guise,
The world transforms before our eyes.
Secrets stir in leaves' soft sway,
In the twilight's caress, we find our way.

Crickets chirp their twilight song,
While shadows stretch, both proud and long.
Each branch adorned with stardust light,
Guiding souls through the velvet night.

The air is thick with whispered lore,
Of ancients and dreams that once were more.
In canopies where ancients dwell,
We listen closely, and stories swell.

Fireflies dance in sparkling glee,
Illuminating the path for thee.
Nature's ballad, sweet and rare,
Threads of magic fill the air.

So pause awhile beneath the grove,
In twilight's hush, our hearts will rove.
For in this hour of blissful trance,
The world reveals its secret dance.

Shadows Play Among the Woodland Spirits

In the quiet woods, where shadows lie,
Whispers echo, and spirits sigh.
Among the trees, in twilight's scheme,
The air thrums softly, a waking dream.

Elusive figures flit and tease,
Dancing lightly on the evening breeze.
With laughter shared, the shadows come,
A sprinkle of magic, a tribal hum.

Moonlight spills on ferny floors,
As woodlands open their ancient doors.
The spirits beckon with inviting grace,
In the heart of the night, we find our place.

Together we sway, joined in their plight,
A tapestry woven from day to night.
In harmony, our souls entwine,
Among the whispers, where shadows shine.

So linger long in the sacred grove,
Let woodland spirits teach and rove.
For in their play, we find what's true,
In the dance of shadows, we'll start anew.

Twilight's Dance in the Heart of the Glade

In twilight's gentle glow, shadows play,
The trees sway softly, as night meets day.
Whispers of magic weave through the air,
A dance of secrets, both precious and rare.

Stars peek through leaves, twinkling bright,
The world holds its breath, in the calming night.
Crickets sing songs, in a lilting tune,
While moonlight spills silver, a soft afternoon.

A brook gurgles softly, in merry delight,
Holding the echoes of dreams, taking flight.
Fireflies flicker, like thoughts in the breeze,
Illuminating paths, with effortless ease.

Stories are woven in the hush of the wood,
Where time stands still, as only it could.
The heart of the glade pulses with grace,
A sanctuary found in this hidden space.

So linger awhile, in this tranquil place,
Where nature and magic find endless embrace.
With every heartbeat, let wonders unfold,
In twilight's dance, where dreams are retold.

Flickering Lights on Ancient Boughs

Beneath the vast sky, ancient boughs sway,
Flickering lights guide the traveler's way.
Like whispers of fairies, they shimmer and glow,
Dancing in rhythms that only they know.

Branches entwined, in a delicate weave,
Holding the stories that the night leaves.
A lantern of hope, in the darkest of hours,
These lights tell of magic, of wild blooming flowers.

In the hush of the evening, soft songs rise,
Echoing gently beneath starlit skies.
Each flicker a promise, a wish on the breeze,
Entwined in the shadows, among rustling leaves.

Paths lightened softly by the glow of the night,
Filling our hearts with pure delight.
As dreams drift like smoke, through the depths of the
trees,
Hope lingers always, carried by the breeze.

So follow the glow, let it guide your heart,
In whispers of night, where all journeys start.
For within this forest, where legends take flight,
We'll find our way home, in the flickering light.

Whispers of Lore in the Enchanted Glens

In enchanted glens where the shadows blend,
Whispers of lore find a voice to send.
Beneath aged branches that cradle the sky,
Stories of old breathe gentle and shy.

Echoes of magic in the rustle of leaves,
Carried on currents, where memory weaves.
A tapestry woven with dreams from the past,
In the heart of the glen, where moments hold fast.

Moonlight spills softly on pathways unknown,
Illuminating secrets, where wild thoughts have grown.
Each twinkling star a guardian's eye,
Watching the mysteries that never will die.

Step lightly, dear wanderer, the air is alive,
With whispers and wonders that strive to survive.
In the embrace of the trees, let your spirit soar,
For the glens hold the magic of lore and much more.

Let the silence of night weave its spell on your soul,
As shadows beckon softly, to make you whole.
For in this enchanted realm, you'll discover your place,
Amongst whispers of lore, in nature's warm embrace.

Green Reveries Amidst the Dreaming Trees

In the heart of the woods, where the green does sigh,
Reveries wander, beneath the vast sky.
Trees stand as guardians, their wisdom runs deep,
Singing of secrets that nature will keep.

Among the soft moss, where silence is wide,
Dreams drift like petals, on the river's tide.
Woven in shadows, the echoes of song,
Call forth the spirits of the ancient and strong.

The brook laughs in whispers, a symphony plays,
A harmony found in the labyrinthine maze.
Ferns unfurl gently, in a dance of delight,
While the soft breath of evening brings dreams to light.

Let your heart wander, in this emerald dream,
Where time is a river, and all is supreme.
The trees embrace stories, both humble and grand,
In green reveries, where peace will expand.

So linger in silence, feel the world's gentle tease,
As magic unfolds amidst the dreaming trees.
For here lies a wonder, a tranquil embrace,
In the heart of the woods, find your sacred space.

Woodland Whispers in Gossamer Night

In twilight's embrace, secrets unfurl,
Where shadows dance and shadows swirl.
The moonlight bathes the forest floor,
In whispers soft, ancient tales soar.

Crisp leaves crackle, a symphony sweet,
As fireflies waltz to a magical beat.
Beneath the stars, dreams take their flight,
In the hush of the woodland, cloaked in night.

A silver brook sings a lullaby clear,
Drawing close all who venture near.
Its waters glisten, a liquid star,
In this enchanted realm, just as we are.

With every rustle, a story unfolds,
Of mythical creatures and wonders untold.
The air is thick with a spell so divine,
Ethereal moments where hearts intertwine.

Though dawn soon approaches, we'll linger still,
In the magic of night, our hearts to fulfill.
For woodland whispers will forever remain,
In the depth of the soul, their soft refrain.

Enchanted Voices Beneath the Canopy

Beneath the boughs of emerald light,
Voices twirl in the hush of night.
With every breath, the world seems to sway,
In rhythms of nature, come out to play.

A rustling breeze carries laughter low,
While fireflies shimmer with a gentle glow.
Ferns unfurl like secrets in the dark,
Inviting wanderers, igniting a spark.

The canopy thickens, a guardian strong,
Where dreams flit and flutter, where faeries belong.
A chorus of crickets, their nightly refrain,
Weaves through the silence, a soft, sweet chain.

As starlight dapples the forest wide,
Enchanted voices in shadows confide.
With every rustle, their stories reborn,
In tales of the moon and the dew-kissed morn.

So come, brave hearts, let your spirits twine,
With the whispers of magic, a world so divine.
In the depths of the woodland, let dreams take flight,
And dance in the echoes of the moon's gentle light.

Timeless Echoes of Mossy Dreams

In the cradle of moss, where memories bloom,
Time drifts like petals, dispelling the gloom.
Echoes of laughter, like ripples on streams,
Bathe the cool air, igniting lost dreams.

Great oaks stand guard, their stories entwined,
In marches of seasons, the past is defined.
With barks like parchment, ancient and wise,
Whisper the lore held beneath starry skies.

A carpet of leaves is where spirits play,
Each step taken softens the weight of the day.
With every breath, the woodland seems near,
Timeless and patient, forever sincere.

The scent of the earth after rain's gentle kiss,
Keeps dreams wrapped in magic, so fragile, so blissed.
In the hush of the twilight, when shadows convene,
Life's stories entwine on the mossy scene.

So linger awhile in this velvet embrace,
Where nature is woven, a warm, tender space.
Feel the heartbeat of earth in the silence around,
In timeless echoes, true magic is found.

Celestial Glimmers in Hallowed Groves

In hallowed groves, where the starlight weaves,
Glimmers of magic entwine with the leaves.
Each branch a story, each root a thread,
Binding the living with the gentle dead.

Moonbeams drape like silks, soft and sweet,
Upon the earth's canvas, where shadows meet.
A silvery glow dances on the stream,
In the hallowed silence, we float like a dream.

Whispers of starlight brush against skin,
Embracing the night as though it begins.
And creatures unseen rustle through the mist,
In the magical hush, not a moment is missed.

Awake with the fireflies, illuminating gloom,
Creating a world full of wonder and bloom.
Where each spark ignites a flicker of hope,
In this sacred enclave, here we will cope.

So wander with me through the glimmering scenes,
In the embrace of the grove, we'll gather our dreams.
Under celestial wonders, hearts open wide,
In this hallowed haven, let magic be our guide.

Glowing Trails of Whimsy and Wonder

In the twilight's gentle loom,
Where magic weaves its spell,
Footsteps light on paths of gleam,
With secrets yet to tell.

Fireflies dance in playful swirls,
As laughter fills the air,
With every twinkle, hope unfurls,
To banish whispers of despair.

Beneath the arch of starlit skies,
Imagination takes its flight,
Holding dreams in open eyes,
Embracing all the night.

Each breeze whispers tales anew,
Of journeys yet to be,
Woven soft in silver dew,
As hearts roam wild and free.

So join the chase, the vibrant chase,
Through glades of rich delight,
For in this realm, there's boundless space,
To craft your own moonlight.

Veils of Radiance in the Sylvan Breeze

In ancient woods where shadows play,
A radiant path unfolds,
With whispers of the breaking day,
And sunlight's golden molds.

The leaves sway gently in the sigh,
Of secrets drifting low,
As creatures grant a knowing eye,
To everything in tow.

With petals soft like silken threads,
And blooms that hold the sun,
Each step a tale that nature spreads,
Of journeys just begun.

The songs of streams in crystal tones,
Are echoes of the past,
In this domain where magic roams,
Eternally steadfast.

So breathe the air of fleeting time,
Where dreams and forests blend,
In sylvan realms, a soothing rhyme,
Where hearts and nature mend.

Fables Found in the Grove's Embrace

Beneath the boughs of ageless trees,
Fables softly lie,
In every whisper of the breeze,
A world where spirits fly.

The bark, a canvas rich and wise,
Holds tales of ancient lore,
While golden light in laughter sighs,
Through every open door.

With every footprint on the grass,
New stories intertwine,
As sunlight through the branches pass,
The heart and soul align.

So wander in this enchanted place,
Where magic intertwines,
The grove will wrap you in its grace,
As life in beauty shines.

Seek not the end, but the delight,
In tales that come alive,
For fables found in morning light,
Will always help you thrive.

Dreamlike Interludes of Earth and Sky

In twilight's hush where worlds collide,
The earth and sky embrace,
With stars that beckon from their ride,
In an ethereal space.

Clouds drift soft like whispered dreams,
Across the moon's pale face,
While rivers hum their gentle themes,
In nature's warm embrace.

The mountains stand like silent guards,
Their peaks in twilight glow,
Each stone a tale, each yard a shard,
Of wonders yet to know.

With every breeze that softly calls,
The heart begins to soar,
In dreamlike hues, where magic sprawls,
To offer evermore.

So reach beyond the here and now,
In realms where dreams can fly,
For life's a canvas, vast and wow,
In the dance of earth and sky.

Floating Thoughts in the Faerie Garden

In the glen where faeries dwell,
Whispers dance in magic's spell.
Petals drift like dreams at play,
Touching hearts in soft array.

Glimmers spark on leafy boughs,
Shimmering like secret vows.
Giggles echo through the air,
Joyful spirits, light as air.

Mirthful songs the nightingale sings,
While the moonlight gently clings.
Clouds like whispers float above,
Casting shadows, wrapping love.

Underneath the starlit skies,
Hope and laughter gently rise.
In the garden, time stands still,
Floating thoughts, a tranquil thrill.

Every moment, pure delight,
Captured in the silver light.
Hearts unbound, together we,
Dance upon life's tapestry.

Serene Play of Light Among Twisting Vines

Sunbeams filter through the leaves,
Where the creeping ivy weaves.
Golden drops on emerald hue,
Nature's brush paints all anew.

Gently swaying in the breeze,
Vines embrace like happy trees.
Each ray casts a playful glint,
Where shadows flicker, softly hint.

In the twilight's tender grace,
Light and dark begin to chase.
While the petals pulse and sway,
In a dance of night and day.

Crickets sing their twilight tune,
Beneath the watchful, crescent moon.
Every moment feels like flight,
In this serene play of light.

Whispers echo, secrets old,
Stories through the ages told.
Among the vines, hope takes its throne,
In this place where dreams have grown.

The Language of Leaves Whispering Softly

In the forest, leaves converse,
Hidden tales in trees rehearsed.
Rustling softly in the breeze,
Shared like secrets 'neath the trees.

A gentle touch, the branches sway,
Nature speaks in her own way.
Golden hues and emerald shades,
Life's tapestry gracefully fades.

When the rain begins to fall,
Leaves collect the droplets small.
In their dance, they glide and slide,
Waving as the storms subside.

Each whisper holds a fleeting thought,
Silent lessons subtly wrought.
The language flows through roots and vine,
Connecting all with love's design.

In every breath, the world does sing,
Harmonies that nature brings.
Listen close, let your heart seek,
The whispers that the leaves do speak.

Enigmas Veiled in the Misty Grove

Through the fog, a figure glides,
Where ancient secrets often bide.
Shadows dance on twisted paths,
In the mist, the quiet laughs.

Echoes of what once was known,
In the air, a mystery grown.
Veiled in silver, soft and clear,
Every step whispers 'draw near.'

Flickering lights, a lantern's glow,
Guiding hearts where few dare go.
Misty fingers entwine the night,
Leading souls toward the light.

In the grove, the secrets blend,
Fog and twilight smoothly mend.
Every shadow, every hue,
Holds the promise of the true.

Cloaked in wonder, hearts abide,
Mysteries we cannot hide.
In the mist, we seek and roam,
Finding in the enigma, home.

9 781805 628934